ILLUSTRATED BIOGRAPHY FOR KIDS

LEONARDO DA VINCI

EXTRAORDINARY SCIENTIST

WHO CHANGED THE WORLD

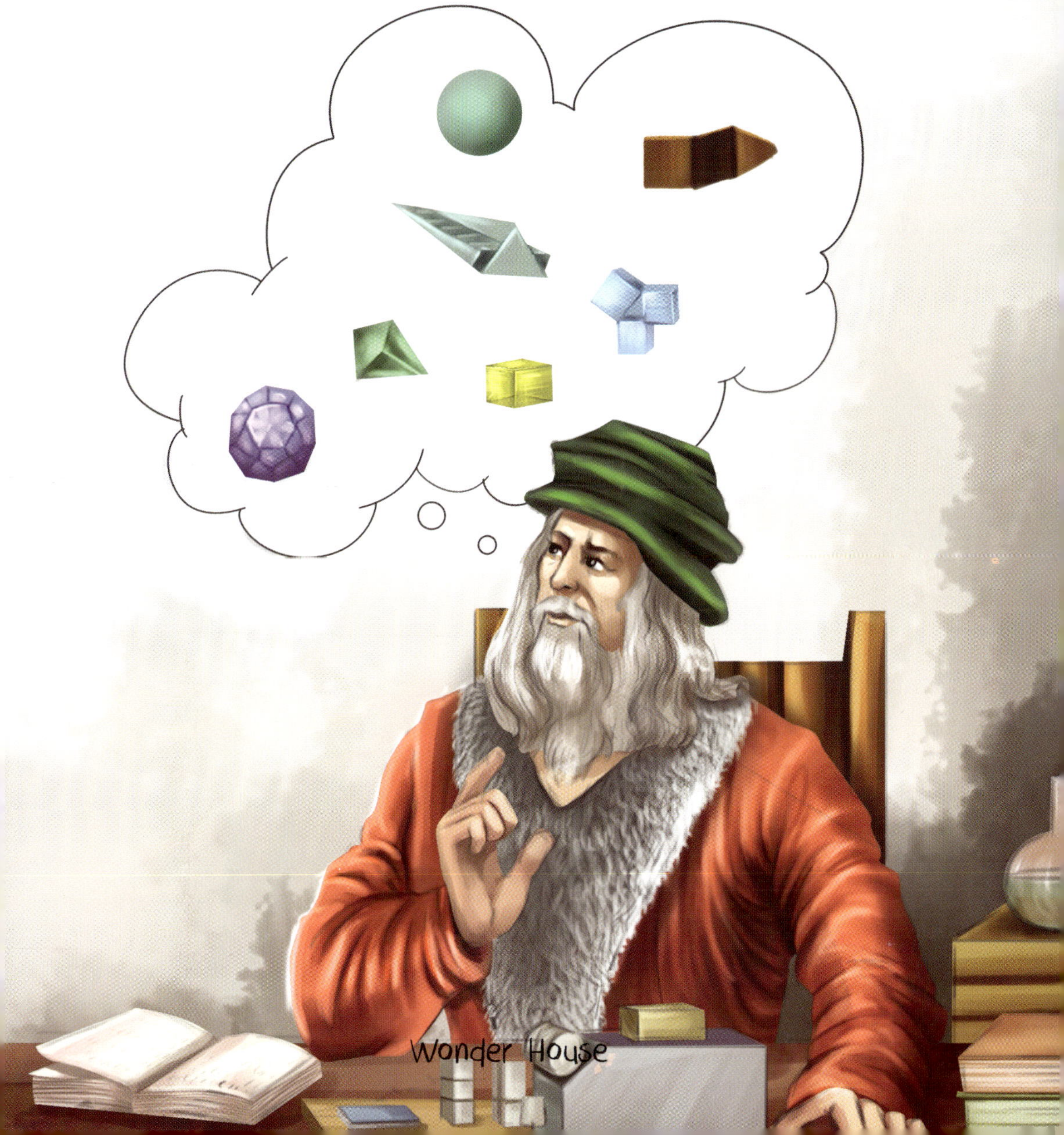

Wonder House

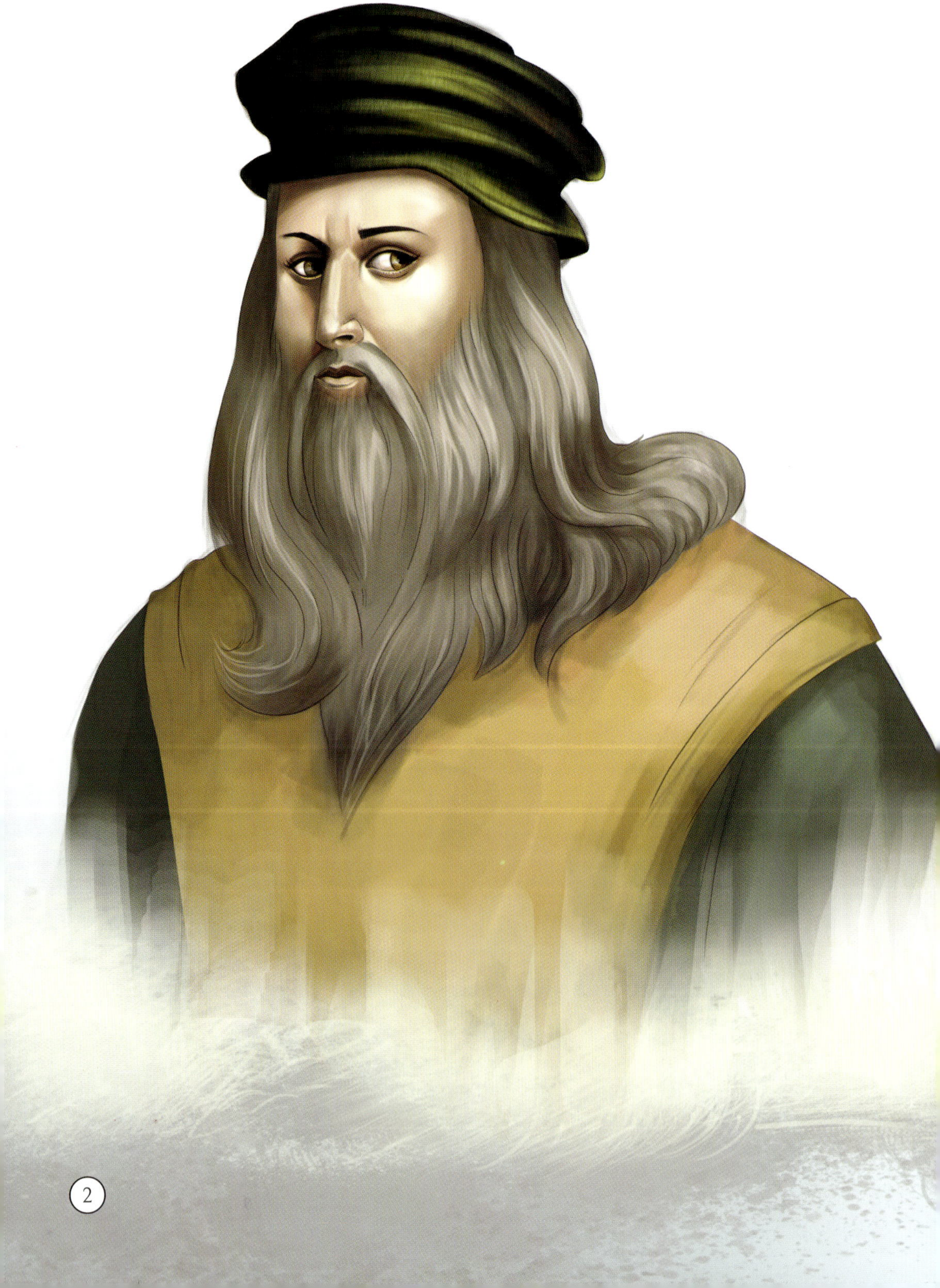

THE RENAISSANCE MAN

Leonardo da Vinci (1452-1519) was an Italian Polymath. He was an ingenious painter, inventor, sculptor, engineer, artist and an outstanding architect. As a man blessed with an inquisitive mind and sharp intellect, his interest varied a great deal. He indulged himself in the studies of several disciplines ranging from arts, science, nature and mathematics, which greatly influenced his work. His diverse interest and natural genius epitomized him as a true Renaissance man in all forms and glory. His exemplary designs, innovative techniques and extraordinary vision has been a guiding light for artists and scientists for centuries, and holds relevance even till today.

EARLY LIFE

Leonardo da Vinci was born on 15 April 1452, in the village of Anchiano in Tuscany, Italy. He was born out of wedlock to a Ser Piero da Vinci, a notary and Caterina, a young peasant woman. He grew up at his father's estate in the town of Vinci, where he spent his childhood with his uncle and grandparents.

He didn't receive any formal education beyond basic reading, writing, and arithmetic but his artistic inclinations were identified at a very

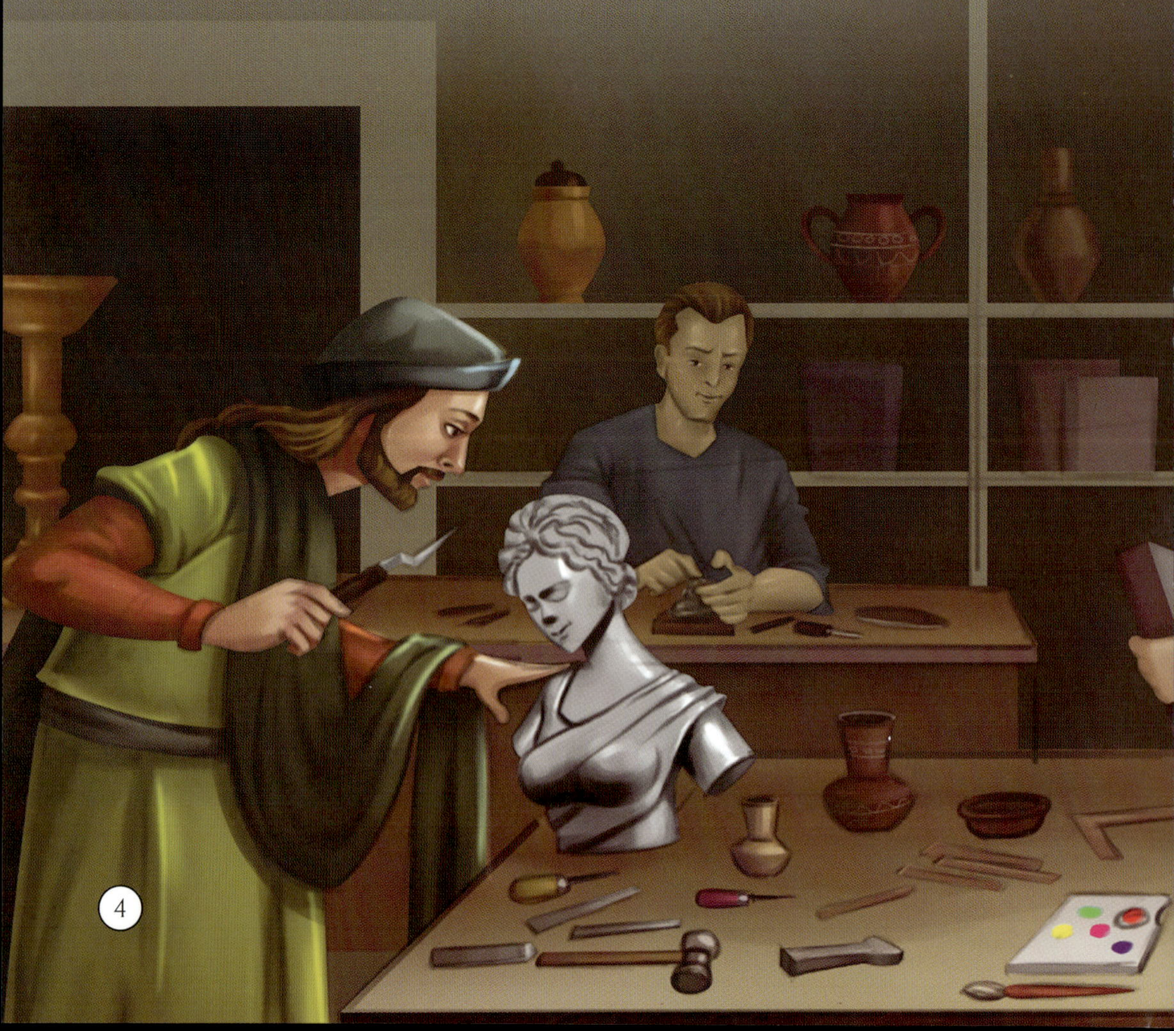

young age. At the age of 15, he started his apprenticeship with the noted sculptor and painter Andrea del Verrocchio of Florence.

During his apprenticeship, he developed his skills in drawing, painting, and sculpting; and alongside gained in-depth knowledge in other diverse fields such as metallurgy, hydraulics, carpentry, anatomy and architecture.

THE JOURNEY BEGINS

In 1472, Leonardo was offered membership in the Guild of Saint Luke, the famous guild of painters and other artists, but he continued to work with Verrocchio till he became an independent artist in 1478. It is believed that da Vinci helped his master Verrocchio complete the *Baptism of Christ* around 1475. Historians claim that the work done by da Vinci was so superior that Verrocchio gave up painting altogether, and never picked up a paintbrush again.

Da Vinci received his first independently commissioned work in 1478. He was appointed to paint the altarpiece for St. Bernard in the Palazzo Vecchio. Later in march 1481, he was commissioned by the monks of San Donato in Scopeto to paint *The Adoration of the Magi*. However, both the commissions remained unfinished as Leonardo soon left the city for better opportunities.

BACK ON THE ROAD

Da Vinci's earliest known work dates back to 1473, when he drew a pen-and-ink landscape drawing of Arno valley. It is believed that he was among the first to suggest, the usage of Arno valley as a navigable channel between Florence and Pisa.

In 1482, he entered into the service of the Duke of Milan, Ludovico Sforza. He spent seventeen years in his service. During these years Leonardo cultivated his artistic and scientific skills that helped him reach new heights in the realm of artistic world. It was here that he was commissioned to paint *The Last Supper*, for the dining hall of the monastery of Santa Maria delle Grazie along with *The Virgin of the Rocks*.

In Milan, da Vinci was employed with a number of projects for the Sforza family. One of the most celebrated one was the huge equestrian monument of Francesco Sforza, Ludovico Sforza's predecessor. This equestrian monument was to be casted in bronze and was planned grandly. It was deemed to surpass all equestrian statues of the time in both size and grandeur. Leonardo completed the clay structure of the base form and made detailed plans for its casting.

Unfortunately, the bronze earmarked for it was used in making canons in order to defend the city against the French invasion. The clay statue laid was also destroyed during the war.

In the aftermath of the French defeat of Milan, da Vinci with his assistant Salai left for Venice, where he indulged in various architectural and engineering marvels and made extensive plans to defend the city from possible military and navy attacks.

ESTABLISHING HIS LEGACY

In 1502, da Vinci served as a military architect and engineer to the Cesare Borgia, the son of Pope Alexander VI, where he made a town plan for Imola, and earned the patronage of Cesare. During his patronage, he traveled throughout Italy and enhanced his knowledge by examining nature and people. He carried his journals and books along with him to compile his ideas and observations.

He returned to Florence in 1503, and began working on his most famous work, the portrait of *Lisa del Giocondo*, or the *Mona Lisa*. He continued to work upon it till the later years of his life. In 1506, he was summoned to Milan, where he was commissioned some portraits on behalf of the king of France, Louis XII.

In 1515, after King Francis I of France recaptured Milan, Leonardo was again called into the service of the French king. He was conferred the title of chief architect, painter, engineer, and mechanic to the king.

Francis I permitted him to use the manor house of Clos Lucé. Leonardo spent his last three years here, in the company of his friend and apprentice, Francesco Melzi.

During this time his profound knowledge of mechanics and engineering reached its zenith. In these last few years, Leonardo drew plans for the castle town in Romorantin, which the king intended to erect. He even went on to make a mechanical lion, which could walk and make its chest open when struck with a wand, revealing his heart filled with a bunch of lilies.

BIG BRAIN ETERNAL IDEAS

During his apprenticeship in Verrocchio's workshop, Leonardo began his studies of anatomy and the human body. His drawings and notations of human skeletons, muscles, tendons, vessels, and other physical features were far ahead of his time. Besides humans he also made a detailed study of the anatomical structure of animals such as monkeys, frogs, birds, and horses.

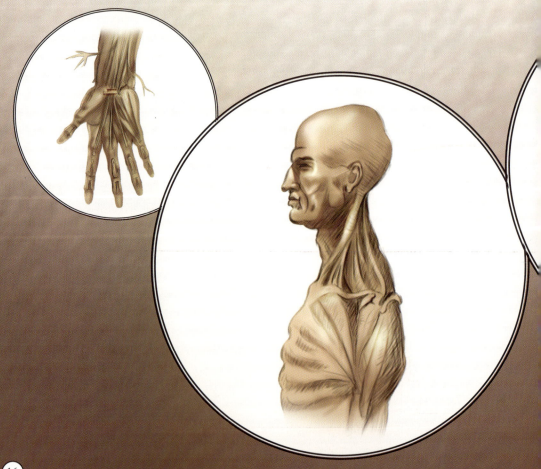

Leonardo's in-depth study of muscles, nerves, and vascular systems helped him to construe the physiology and the mechanics of movement, which later found expression in his art work. Unfortunately, he never published his drawings and discoveries, otherwise who knows what door of possibilities it would have opened in the advances of medical science.

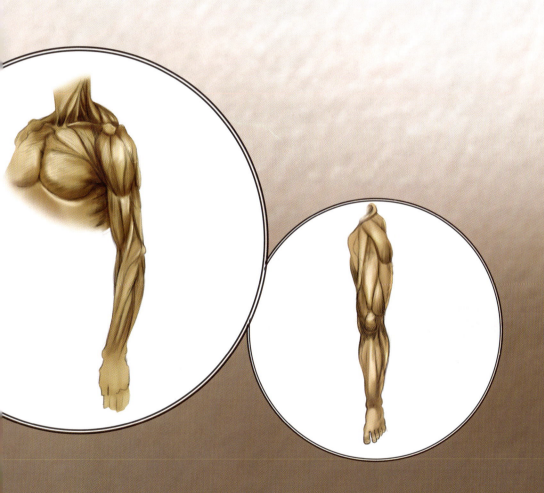

Da Vinci was a proficient engineer and a skilled inventor. He studied and designed many machines and devices for the protection of the state against siege or outside aggression. During his time in Venice, he planned a system of movable barricades to protect the city against any possible foreign attack.

His journals are filled with the treasures of his imaginative designs of futuristic inventions, both practical as well as impractical. These designs include musical instruments, steam cannons, mechanical

devices, hydraulic pumps, and many more. Using his inventive mind, da Vinci sketched war machines, devices to concentrate solar power, calculators, and even conceptualized early models of the helicopter.

FROM THE CANON OF MASTER
THE LAST SUPPER

The Last Supper, was painted by Leonardo during his time in Milan. The painting measures about 181 by 346 inches and is the artist's only surviving fresco. It very well captures the moment, when Jesus tells his twelve apostles over the passover dinner that 'One of you will betray me.' The peculiar reaction of the apostles conveyed by their distinctive body language is one of the most captivating features of the painting.

However, the composition of Jesus in the center surrounded by his apostles, depicting his oneness as well as isolation from others, has influenced artists and painters for generations. Instead of using the reliable fresco technique, Leonardo painted *The Last Supper*, on the dried surface which has led to its early deterioration. Fortunately, with the usage of modern techniques and proper restoration, this masterpiece has survived the tide of time.

MONA LISA

Painted between 1503-1506, the portrait of *La Gioconda*, popularly known as *Mona Lisa* is housed at the Louvre Museum in Paris, France. It is considered as one of the most famous and expensive paintings in the world.

The renowned painting known for its elusive smile, awe-inspiring composition, subtle forms, and the illusionary landscape has puzzled historians for centuries. The usage of sfumato technique, i.e., the absence

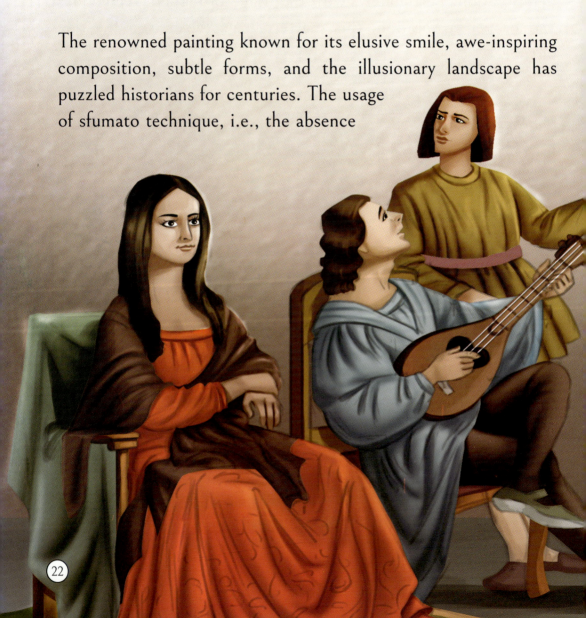

of sharp lines, gave the portrait a much more realistic look. Da Vinci played with light and shadows, especially around the eyes and the corner of the mouth to bring the mysterious qualities to the painting.

The painting also portrays a sense of harmony between nature and humanity, which reflects da Vinci's idea of an eternal link between the two. Da Vinci extensively used his anatomical knowledge to create an image which is highly realistic and expressive. This naturalistic approach finds its expression in *Mona Lisa*.

VITRUVIAN MAN

The *Vitruvian man* depicts da Vinci's notion of the perfect human proportions, where a man is depicted in two superimposed positions in a circle and a square with arms and legs spread wide apart. Leonardo believed that the working of the human body is in correspondence with the working of nature. This ink and paper drawing represents his in-depth understanding of nature, mathematics, and art, which he blended very well in his works.

SALVATOR MUNDI

The painting depicts Jesus Christ in a Renaissance blue robes, where the one hand is raised in benediction, while the other is holding a transparent non-refracting crystal orb, representing the celestial world. After its rediscovery and proper restoration, the painting was exhibited at the National Gallery, London in 2011–12. The painting in 2017 was sold at a public auction for a whopping US$450.3 million. Since then it has been titled as the most expensive painting ever sold in a public auction.

APPROACH TO LIFE

Da Vinci considered art and science as interdependent upon each other. Instead of treating them as separate distinct field of studies, he believed that one cannot be excelled without the help of the other.

His curiosity to learn from these different fields led him to master several disciplines ranging from engineering, mathematics, anatomy, sculpting, and painting. He believed in the interconnectedness of all these subjects and worked to gain an in-depth knowledge of them. This maybe the reason why he failed to complete a considerable number of paintings and projects during his lifetime.

He spent a majority of his time with nature, and studied scientific laws. He maintained journals and diaries, while employing himself in a great deal of thinking and writing, about the observations made and ideas constructed.

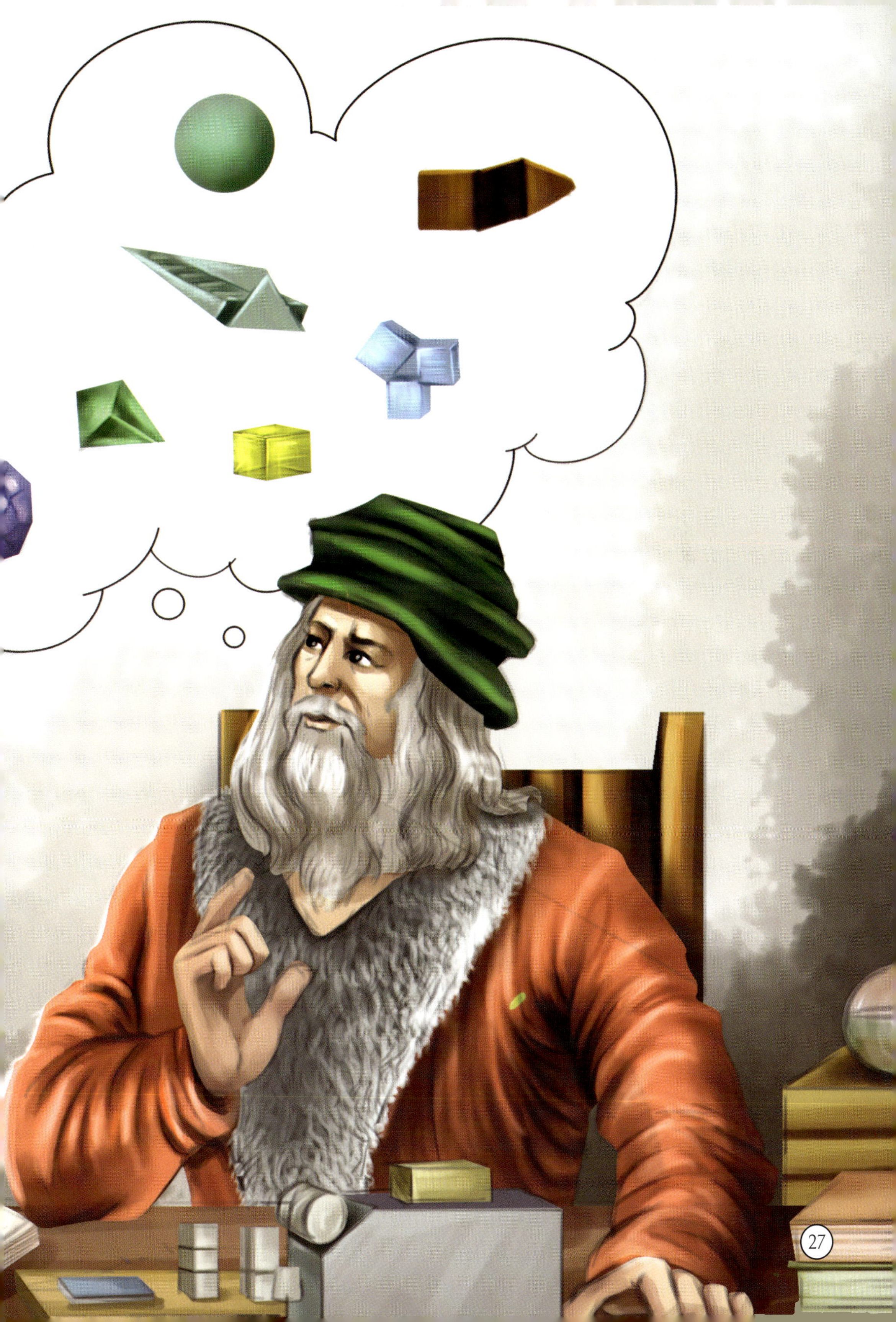

TWILIGHT DAYS

Da Vinci spent his last years in the Clos Lucé, near Amboise in France. It is widely believed that Leonardo completed his last painting, *St. John the Baptist* here, which showcases his supremacy of the Sfumoto technique.

It is believed that Leonardo died of stroke on 2 May 1519 at the age of 67. He was buried in the church of Saint Florentin, which was badly damaged during the French Revolution. The site was completely razed in the early nineteenth century, since then it has been impossible for historians to identify the last remains of Leonardo da Vinci.

AN UNFORGETTABLE MAN

Leonardo da Vinci was an influential figure in the Renaissance, his unprecedented achievements as an engineer, artist, sculptor, and inventor left an eternal mark on the world. He left behind an everlasting legacy of some of the greatest art works and inventions which were not only way ahead of his time but hold relevance even till today.

To this day, *Mona Lisa* is regarded as among the greatest paintings of all time. Every year millions of tourists visit Paris to get a glimpse of master's famous artwork.

Just like literature cannot be talked about, without mentioning the Immortal Bard, Shakespeare, similarly discussions about art remain hollow without the mention of the Renaissance Man, Leonardo da Vinci.

1452 : Birth of Renaissance artist and scientist Leonardo da Vinci

1464 : Enrollment as an apprentice in the workshop of Andrea del Verrocchio in Florence

1472 : Completes his apprenticeship as an artist in Florence

1482 : Moves to Milan where he works for Ludovico Sforza

1498 : Leonardo da Vinci completes his wall mural *The Last Supper* in Milan's Sante Maria delle Grazie

1500 : Leonardo da Vinci visits Venice

1502 : Moves to Rome and starts to work for Cesare Borgia to sort out the city's canals

1503-1506 : Leonardo da Vinci completes his painting the *Mona Lisa*

1517 : Moves to France to work for Francis I of France

1519 : Leonardo da Vinci dies at Clos Lucé in France

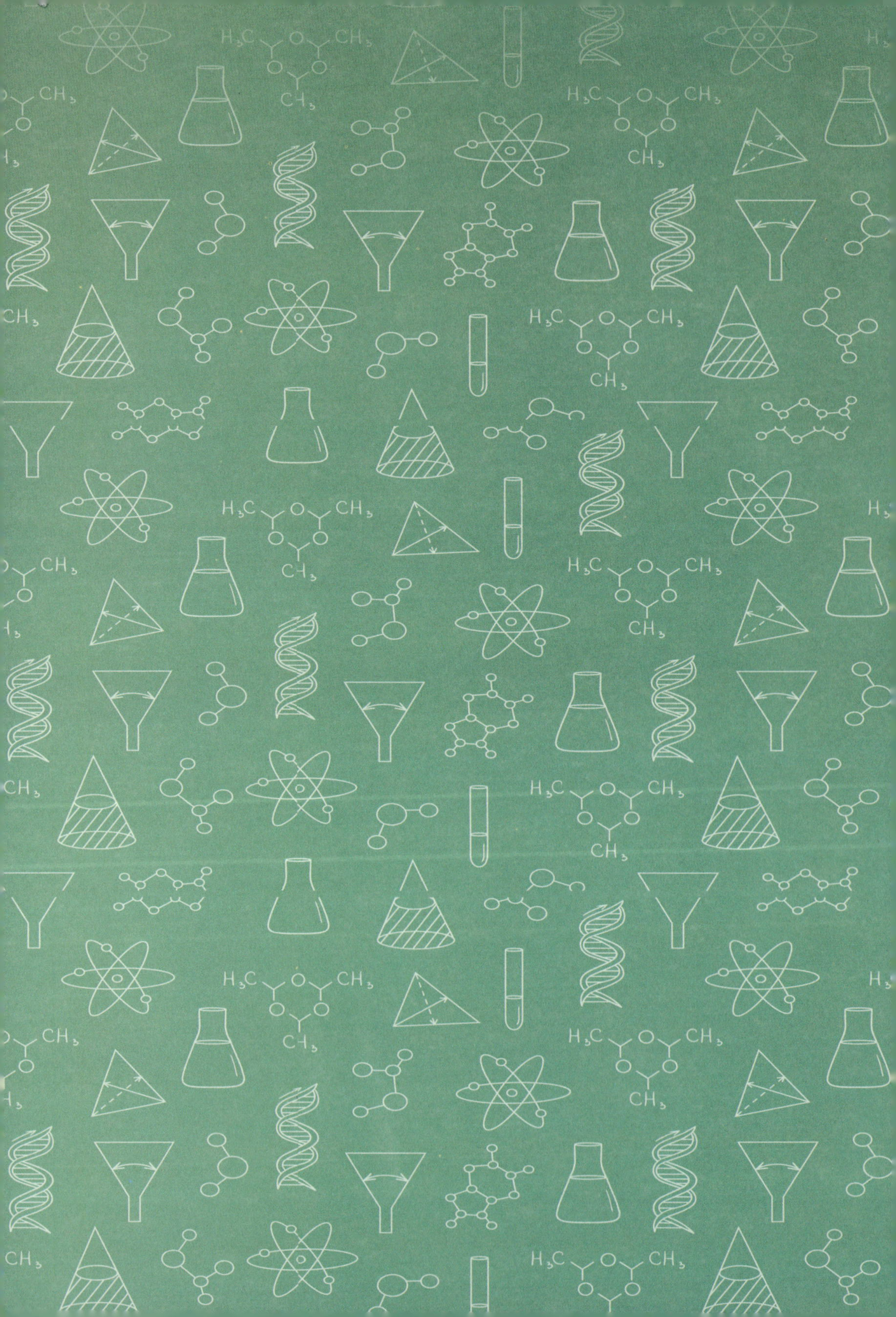